AF270416

# PHILADELPHIA PHILLIES

BY ANTHONY K. HEWSON

SportsZone

An Imprint of Abdo Publishing
abdobooks.com

abdobooks.com

Published by Abdo Publishing, a division of ABDO, PO Box 398166, Minneapolis, Minnesota 55439. Copyright © 2023 by Abdo Consulting Group, Inc. International copyrights reserved in all countries. No part of this book may be reproduced in any form without written permission from the publisher. SportsZone™ is a trademark and logo of Abdo Publishing.

Printed in China.
102022
012023

Cover Photo: Dustin Bradford/Icon Sportswire/AP Images
Interior Photos: Michael Reaves/Getty Images Sport/Getty Images, 4; APA/Archive Photos/Getty Images, 7; George Rinhart/Corbis Historical/Getty Images, 9, 12; Mark Rucker/Transcendental Graphics/Getty Images Sport/Getty Images, 11; Bettmann/Getty Images, 14; AP Images, 17, 21, 24; MLB Photos/Getty Images, 18; Focus on Sport/Getty Images Sport/Getty Images, 22; Tony Tomsic/AP Images, 26; Focus on Sport/Getty Images, 28, 31; Sporting News/Getty Images, 32; Mitchell Layton/Getty Images Sport/Getty Images, 35; Frank Franklin II/AP Images, 37; Julie Jacobson/AP Images, 39; Rich Graessle/Icon Sportswire/Getty Images, 41

Editor: Charlie Beattie
Series Designer: Becky Daum

**Library of Congress Control Number: 2022940483**

**Publisher's Cataloging-in-Publication Data**

Names: Hewson, Anthony K., author.
Title: Philadelphia Phillies / by Anthony K. Hewson
Description: Minneapolis, Minnesota: Abdo Publishing, 2023 | Series: Inside MLB | Includes online resources and index.
Identifiers: ISBN 9781098290283 (lib. bdg.) | ISBN 9781098275488 (ebook)
Subjects: LCSH: Philadelphia Phillies (Baseball team)--Juvenile literature. | Baseball teams--Juvenile literature. | Professional sports--Juvenile literature. | Sports franchises--Juvenile literature. | Major League Baseball (Organization)--Juvenile literature.
Classification: DDC 796.35764--dc23

# CONTENTS

# CHAPTER 1

# A QUAKING START

Bryce Harper stepped into the batter's box in the bottom of the eighth inning of Game 5 in the 2022 National League Championship Series (NLCS). His Philadelphia Phillies were one win away from a World Series appearance. But they trailed the San Diego Padres 3–2 in the game. When Philadelphia had made Harper the richest free agent signing in baseball three years earlier, it was for moments like this.

Phillies catcher J. T. Realmuto had singled to open the inning. On the mound for San Diego was hard-throwing right-hander Robert Suarez. The left-handed hitting Harper had 15 of his 18 home runs during the regular season against right-handed pitchers.

Bryce Harper hit six home runs during the 2022 postseason.

After six pitches of the duel between San Diego's power pitcher and Philadelphia's power hitter, the count stood 2–2. On the seventh pitch, Suarez delivered a 99-mile-per-hour fastball on the outside corner. Harper dropped the barrel of his bat on it and slammed it to deep left-center field. He slowly paced out of the batter's box with his eyes following the ball. Only after it settled in the seats for a two-run, go-ahead homer did Harper start to jog around the bases.

In the stands, the crowd at Citizens Bank Park in Philadelphia screamed with joy. It was the type of moment they had hoped to see from one of the game's biggest stars. And Harper's homer made the difference. Philadelphia's 4–3 lead held. The Phillies were headed to the World Series.



## HUMBLE BEGINNINGS

The World Series was still 20 years away from existence when the Phillies first took the field in 1883. The team formed that year as members of the National League (NL). The nickname came from owner Al Reach, a former player who made a fortune

National League Park, later known as the Baker Bowl, held 12,500 fans when it was first built.

selling sports equipment. He chose it because Philly is a nickname for Philadelphia. Others called the team the Quakers in the early years. However, by 1890 the Phillies nickname was official.

Whatever fans called them, the team didn't do much winning. The Phillies/Quakers won just 17 games in their inaugural 98-game season. Philadelphia's main pitcher, John Coleman, finished with a record of 12–48 in an era when pitchers threw far more often than in the modern game.

## BUILDING

Starting in 1887, the Phillies played home games at National League Park, later known as the Baker Bowl. After a fire

## STADIUM TRAGEDY



destroyed the wooden ballpark in 1894, it was rebuilt using modern steel and brick for construction. It also featured a brand-new construction technique with an upper seating level that hung over the lower level, bringing fans closer to the action. The result was one of the best stadiums of the era.

Despite the team's struggles on the field during its first season, Philadelphia still had a handful of great players in those early years. In an era when players hit few home runs, some Phillies were the exception. Sam Thompson was one of the best power hitters of his era. In 1889 he led the NL with 20 homers.

Still, the Phillies rarely were contenders. From 1883 to 1914, the team often had more wins than losses but usually finished far back in the standings. However, Philadelphia was ready to break through in 1915.

## THE PHILLIES' FIRST WORLD SERIES

Pitcher Grover Cleveland Alexander came to the Phillies as a rookie in 1911. With an arsenal of moving pitches and great control, Alexander led the NL in wins in his first season. By 1915 he led the league not only in victories but also in earned-run average (ERA), innings, and strikeouts.

The 1915 Phillies led the NL for most of the season. Outfielder Gavvy Cravath led the NL with 24 homers. Philadelphia went on to win the NL by seven games and reached its first World Series.

Gavvy Cravath led the NL in home runs six times in seven seasons from 1913 to 1919.

Alexander took the mound in Game 1. He kept the Boston Red Sox scoreless for seven innings, but the Phillies managed just one run of their own. The Red Sox tied the game in the eighth.

Philadelphia came right back and loaded the bases. Cravath grounded out, but a run scored to take the lead back. First baseman Fred Luderus followed with a run-scoring single. Alexander closed it out from there to give the Phillies a 1–0 start.

That was the only game in the series decided by more than one run. Unfortunately for the Phillies, they were on the losing end the rest of the way. Boston scored the winning run in the ninth inning of both Game 2 and Game 3. In Game 5, the Phillies led 4–2 after seven innings as Luderus had three runs batted in (RBIs). But the Phillies blew the lead and the series in a 5–4 loss.

## END OF AN ERA

The Phillies made their first World Series under owner William Baker, who had taken over the team two years earlier. It was Baker's name that went on the Phillies' home ballpark. But while the Phillies had immediate success under Baker, he was not that interested in baseball.

Baker had said his hope as a team owner was to sell the Phillies and make a profit. He didn't want to spend a lot of money. To sell more tickets, Baker allowed fans to stand in a roped-off area on the field in the 1915 World Series. Three balls in Game 5 were hit into this area, resulting in easy home runs for the Red Sox.

Baker's biggest mistake was trading Alexander in 1917. The star pitcher was due a big raise on a new contract that Baker did not want to pay. He traded the ace to the Chicago Cubs for $60,000 and two players.

Grover Cleveland Alexander set a modern rookie record by winning 28 games in 1911.

Baker also moved other stars in order to raise more money. All the moves sent the Phillies tumbling into last place. They remained near the bottom of the NL for decades to come.

# THE WHIZ KIDS

The trade of Grover Cleveland Alexander was not the only reason for the Phillies' decline. But there is no question that the trade of Alexander came right before the worst 30 years in Phillies history.

From 1918 to 1948, the team finished last in the eight-team NL 16 times. Philadelphia lost 100 or more games 12 times. It took until 1932 for the Phillies to post their only winning record during that stretch. They finished 78–76, which was still only good enough to finish fourth. They were 12 games behind the league champion Chicago Cubs.

However, in the middle of all that losing came a few highlights. In 1920 outfielder Cy Williams led the NL with

Phillies outfielder Cy Williams was the first NL player to hit 200 career home runs.

Indiana native Chuck Klein was nicknamed "the Hoosier Hammer" for his hitting ability.

15 homers. In 1923 he'd upped his total to 41. Second-place Jack Fournier hit only 22.

In 1928 the Phillies traded for young right fielder Chuck Klein. In just his second season, the outfielder hit 43 homers, second in baseball only to legendary New York Yankees slugger Babe Ruth. That same year, left fielder Lefty O'Doul won the batting title with a .398 average while also hitting

32 home runs. Klein won the first MVP Award in Phillies history in 1932. The next year, he won the Triple Crown by leading the NL with a .368 batting average, 28  home runs, and 120 RBIs.

Williams, Klein, and O'Doul were all left-handed hitters. That meant they had a big advantage at the Baker Bowl. The right-field fence stood only 272 feet from home plate.

## OWNERSHIP CHANGES

William Baker died in 1930. Control of the team eventually passed to Gerald Nugent, who had worked for the Phillies since 1925. Nugent had deep knowledge of baseball but rarely had the money to improve the club. In some years, the Phillies had barely enough cash to pay for spring training.

Nugent was always looking for ways to improve the team's finances. He needed to sell more tickets, but the team was so bad that fans stayed away. Nugent resorted to selling off the team's best players for cash, including Klein.

One thing Nugent managed to do was get Philadelphia out of the Baker Bowl. The stadium was aging and expensive to keep up. In 1938 the Phillies moved to Shibe Park, the home of their crosstown rivals, the Philadelphia Athletics.

The move did not work out. Still struggling for money, Nugent was out as owner in 1942. Philadelphia's next owner, William Cox, was banned from baseball a year later for betting on his team's games. Eventually, the team was sold to father-and-son duo Bill Carpenter Sr. and Jr. The Carpenters tried everything to turn the Phillies around. One experiment was to leave the team's losing past behind by changing its name in 1944.

The Phillies held a contest to pick a new nickname. "Blue Jays" was the winner. But most fans didn't like or use the name, and it was never made official with the league. By 1948 Philadelphia had given up on the Blue Jays nickname.

## THE CITY SERIES

Interleague play between AL and NL teams began in 1997. Before then, the only time teams from different leagues could meet was in the World Series. However, the Athletics and Phillies did meet in exhibition games throughout the A's years in Philadelphia. The City Series began in 1883. While the games did not count, fans and players took the rivalry seriously. Now, with interleague play, the Phillies and now Oakland A's can meet in the regular season.

## SIGNS OF HOPE

Things like name changes didn't have much effect on fixing the Phillies. What did help was investing in promising young players. That was the job of the younger Carpenter, who served as team president. Carpenter handed out big money to sign center fielder Richie Ashburn and pitcher Robin Roberts. The two future Hall of Famers helped turn the Phillies around.

Richie Ashburn was elected to the Baseball Hall of Fame in 1995, 33 years after he retired as a player.

The 1949 Phillies managed a record of 81–73. That was their best season since 1917. Fans began to sense they might have enough talent to be serious contenders.

Robin Roberts's 3,379 1/3 innings pitched are the most in Phillies history.

Those hopes depended on the young core of players known as "the Whiz Kids." That included players like Ashburn and Roberts, who were both 22, and 20-year-old pitcher Curt Simmons. All were signed and developed through the Phillies' minor league system. Added to that were star veterans like outfielder Dick Sisler and relief pitcher Jim Konstanty, who was the 1950 NL MVP.

The 1950 Phillies raced into first place and led the NL for most of the season. Philadelphia had a seven-game lead with 11 games to go. But the team went into a nosedive, losing eight of 10. Heading into the last game of the season, the Phillies' lead was down to one over the Brooklyn Dodgers. The two teams squared off with the pennant on the line at Ebbets Field in New York.

Roberts, who had won 20 games and was an All-Star, got the start. He and Dodgers starter Don Newcombe each pitched a complete game. Roberts allowed just a single run, but the Phillies managed only one of their own through nine innings.

In the top of the 10th, Roberts helped his own cause with a leadoff single. Another Phillies single put two men on for Sisler. On a 1–2 count, he sent a towering home run to left to give the Phillies a 4–1 lead. Roberts threw only nine pitches in the bottom of the inning. In a pressure spot, he easily retired all three batters he faced to clinch the pennant for Philadelphia.

# TAKING OVER PHILLY

In the 1950 World Series, it was the Whiz Kids against the legends. The New York Yankees had won the AL pennant in three of the past four years and were loaded with future Hall of Famers. With Roberts having pitched 10 innings just three days earlier, Konstanty got the Game 1 start despite being a relief pitcher that season.

Konstanty pitched well, allowing just a single run in eight innings. But Yankees starter Vic Raschi was even better. He shut out the Phillies, and New York won the opener. Roberts got his turn in Game 2 and struck out five in another 10-inning game. But he gave up a home run to legendary outfielder Joe DiMaggio in the top of the 10th and lost 2–1.

Back home in Philadelphia, the home team had a 2–1 lead into the eighth inning of Game 3 but lost 3–2. New York finished off the sweep the next day. Despite the disappointment, it was still a banner year in Philadelphia.

Though the Whiz Kids never managed to win another pennant, the Phillies had taken a hold on the City of Brotherly Love. The team was regularly drawing more fans than the Athletics, who had become one of the AL's worst teams. After the 1954 season, the A's moved to Kansas City, giving the Phillies full use of Shibe Park and making them the only team in town.

Jim Konstanty won 16 games and saved 22 more during his MVP season in 1950.

# THE FIGHTIN' PHILS

**B**y 1961 the Phillies were historically bad. They lost 107 games, including a streak of 23 straight in July and August.

That was the last season for Robin Roberts in a Philadelphia uniform. Richie Ashburn had already moved on to the Chicago Cubs in 1960. The outfielder retired in 1963 and became a radio broadcaster for the Phillies. The other Whiz Kids were gone too. But a new youngster was just getting started.

Third baseman Dick Allen was from a small coal-mining town called Wampum in western Pennsylvania. It took him just three years to reach the majors after Philadelphia signed him out of high school in 1960. He had played only a few games in

Dick Allen hit a career-high 40 home runs for the Phillies in 1966.

Jim Bunning became a US senator in his home state of Kentucky after his 17-year MLB career ended.

1963, so he was still considered a rookie the next season. Allen slugged his way to the NL Rookie of the Year Award. It was the start of a career that saw him become one of the game's most feared power hitters.

Allen joined a team that already had veteran stars like pitcher Jim Bunning. The future Hall of Famer with the sidearm delivery made Phillies history on June 21 by pitching a perfect game in a 6–0 win over the New York Mets.

Allen and Bunning helped manager Gene Mauch's Phillies stay in first place for most of the 1964 season. Philadelphia had a 6 1/2-game lead in the NL with 12 games left. But a 10-game losing streak threw it all away. One of the worst late-season collapses in baseball history became known as the "Phold of '64."

## A NEW HOME

The 1964 season was one of the last competitive years for the Phillies at Shibe Park, which by then had been renamed Connie Mack Stadium. The park was more than 50 years old and was showing signs of age. Without a new one, the Phillies were rumored to be moving out of Philadelphia. The city eventually agreed to help build a stadium that would be shared by the Phillies and pro football's Philadelphia Eagles.

Veterans Stadium was ready for the 1971 season. In the coming decades, multipurpose stadiums went out of style. But "the Vet" was state of the art for its day. It featured seven levels of seating with restaurants and other fan attractions scattered throughout. Both fans and players loved it.

The 1971 season saw another debut. Harry Kalas took over as the team's radio broadcaster. For the next 39 years,

In 15 years with the Phillies, Steve Carlton set team records with 241 wins and 3,031 strikeouts.

Kalas was the beloved voice of the Phillies to fans. His famous phrase, "That ball is outta here!" signaled every Phillies home run.

In 1972 Steve Carlton became the first Phillies pitcher to win the Cy Young Award as the best pitcher in the NL. Carlton's season was truly incredible. Using his signature slider, the lefty picked up 27 victories, even though the Phillies won just 59 total games.

# THE GLORY YEARS

The Phillies may have been bad, but pieces like Carlton and shortstop Larry Bowa were starting to fall into place. The 1973 season saw the breakout of young third baseman Mike Schmidt and catcher Bob Boone.

By 1976 the turnaround was complete. Schmidt led the league in home runs for the third year in a row. The Phillies won their first of three straight NL East Division titles.

The individual awards kept piling up. Carlton won another Cy Young Award in 1977. But the Phillies could not advance in the playoffs. In each season, they were knocked out in the NL Championship Series (NLCS).

In 1979 the Phillies added another key piece to the puzzle. Pete Rose was well on his way to becoming baseball's all-time hit king. He had also helped the Cincinnati Reds win back-to-back World Series in 1975 and 1976. But after 16 years with the Reds, he signed with the Phillies as a free agent. The move paid off a year later.

## THE PHANATIC

In April 1978, the Phillies debuted the "Phillie Phanatic" as the team's new mascot. The fuzzy, green creature quickly became one of the most recognized mascots in all of sports. The Phanatic can often be seen during games playfully taunting umpires and opposing players or playing pranks on fans and stadium workers.

Mike Schmidt led the NL in home runs eight times during his 18-year career.

The Phillies started off slow in 1980 under manager Dallas Green. But they closed on a 15–6 run. Schmidt hit a two-run homer in extra innings to clinch the division with one game left in the season. He was named NL MVP. Carlton went 24–9 to win yet another Cy Young Award.

Philadelphia won Game 1 of the NLCS against the Houston Astros. The next four games all went to extra innings. Houston took Games 2 and 3, while Philadelphia won Game 4. In the decisive Game 5, center fielder Garry Maddox hit an RBI double in the 10th inning to send the Phillies back to the Fall Classic for the first time in 30 years.

The World Series featured more tight games against the AL champion Kansas City Royals. The Phillies took the first two contests. Kansas City bounced back with two wins of its own.

Philadelphia was down 3–2 heading into the top of the ninth in Game 5. Schmidt led off with a single. He then scored on pinch-hitter Del Unser's double to tie the game. Unser eventually moved to third but was still there when second baseman Manny Trillo came up with two outs. He lined an 0–2 pitch up the middle that bounced off Kansas City closer Dan Quisenberry. By the time third baseman George Brett picked up the ball and fired to first, Trillo was safe and Unser had scored the eventual winning run.

## RECORD AUDIENCE

Green had Carlton ready to pitch Game 6 in Philadelphia. The left-hander didn't disappoint, striking out seven while taking the game into the eighth inning. Closer Tug McGraw then came on to finish the game. He allowed three hits, two walks, and a run, but he also got the final six outs. At long last, the Phillies were champions.

## LEGACIES

Schmidt was the World Series MVP in 1980 and then added another regular-season MVP a year later. But the Phillies came up short in the playoffs, losing to the Montreal Expos.

It took until 1983 before Philadelphia reached the World Series again. Maddox got the series off to a good start against the Baltimore Orioles. His solo homer in the top of the eighth was the difference in winning Game 1. But Schmidt struggled at the plate as the Phillies lost the next four.

The 1983 team was filled with aging stars. The 42-year-old Rose left after the season to join the Expos. Carlton was 38. He had won a fourth Cy Young Award in 1982. But after 1984, he never won more than 13 games in a season. He left the Phillies in 1986 as the most accomplished pitcher in franchise history.

Three years later, Schmidt retired. His 548 career home runs ranked seventh in MLB history when he left the game. Philadelphia needed new stars to step up.

Tug McGraw throws his arms up after recording the final out in the clinching Game 6 of the 1980 World Series.

# THE GOLDEN GENERATION

After finishing last in the NL East a year earlier, the 1993 Phillies came up with one of baseball's great turnarounds. Catcher Darren Daulton led the team with 24 homers. Center fielder Lenny Dykstra led the league in walks and hits. First baseman John Kruk, third baseman Dave Hollins, infielder Mariano Duncan, and outfielder Pete Incaviglia all drove in at least 70 runs. Tommy Greene, Danny Jackson, Curt Schilling, and Terry Mulholland formed a deep pitching rotation. Closer Mitch "Wild Thing" Williams saved 43 games.

The team was most known for its appearance. With beards and mullet haircuts, the Phillies were the shaggiest-looking

First baseman John Kruk was one of the key hitters in the Phillies' "Macho Row" lineup that took the team to the 1993 World Series.

team in baseball. The players basked in the image. Eventually they picked up the nickname "Macho Row."

Fans loved it. More than 3 million packed the Vet as Philadelphia reached the World Series against the defending champion Toronto Blue Jays. While the Phillies eventually lost, it was a memorable showdown. In Game 6, Toronto outfielder Joe Carter hit a series-winning walk-off home run to shut down Macho Row. That was only the second time in history the World Series ended on a walk-off homer.

## GOODBYE TO THE VET

The Macho Row crew was fun, but they didn't stay together long. The team didn't have another winning season until 2001. Former shortstop Larry Bowa returned to Philadelphia as manager. He inherited a team that had stars like third baseman Scott Rolen and outfielder Bobby Abreu. Right behind them were younger, promising players. Shortstop Jimmy Rollins led the NL in stolen bases as a rookie in 2001. Left fielder Pat Burrell started an eight-year streak of 20-homer seasons.

The Phillies' main problem was the Atlanta Braves. Since the teams had been placed in the NL East together in 1994, Atlanta had won the division every year. And that streak continued through 2005. Atlanta fell off in 2006, but the New York Mets jumped ahead of the Phillies.

Scott Rolen was the 1997 NL Rookie of the Year and won three Gold Gloves at third base while playing for the Phillies.

The team did have one shining moment—it opened a new ballpark. Baseball teams had been moving out of multisport stadiums for cozier baseball-only ballparks since the early 1990s. The Phillies joined in on the trend by opening Citizens Bank Park in 2004. Local fans had always referred to the old stadium as "the Vet." They kept that same spirit alive in the new home. Fans quickly dubbed the new park "the Bank."

## HOME COOKING

By the 2007 season, the Phillies were ready to take over the NL East. New manager Charlie Manuel had a lineup of homegrown stars. Rollins and Burrell had now been joined by second baseman Chase Utley, a fan favorite who debuted in 2003 and quickly became an All-Star. First baseman Ryan Howard was NL Rookie of the Year in 2005 after hitting 22 home runs and driving in 63 despite playing only 88 games. Howard's rapid rise continued in 2006. He led the league with 58 homers and 149 RBIs while being named the team's first MVP since Mike Schmidt in 1986.

In 2007 Rollins won the MVP. The Phillies rallied to top the Mets on the season's final day. The division title sent Philadelphia to the playoffs for the first time since Macho Row went to the World Series in 1993. However, the Phillies' new stars didn't last long. They suffered a three-game sweep at the

Jimmy Rollins, *left*, and Chase Utley, *right*, were two of the stars that helped the Phillies win the 2008 World Series.

hands of the Colorado Rockies in the NL Division Series (NLDS). The Phillies hit a combined .172 in the three losses.

A year later, the Phillies again chased down the Mets in September to win the division. But this time they made a longer playoff stay. Philadelphia lost only two games in the first two rounds against the Milwaukee Brewers and Los Angeles Dodgers. The AL champion Tampa Bay Rays waited in the World Series.

# WORTH THE WAIT

The two teams played out a tight series. Phillies ace Cole Hamels, another homegrown talent, pitched seven strong innings in a 3–2 Game 1 win. Tampa Bay tied things up with a close win in Game 2.

The series shifted to Philadelphia for Game 3. The Phillies' starter was 45-year-old Philadelphia native Jamie Moyer. He had skipped school in 1980 to watch the team's victory parade. Now he had a chance to thrill the home crowd again. Moyer took a 4–1 lead into the seventh inning, but the Rays rallied. The game went to the bottom of the ninth tied 4–4.

The Phillies loaded the bases with nobody out for catcher Carlos Ruiz. The righty hit a chopper halfway up the third-base line. Eric Bruntlett beat the throw home to win the game. Ruiz's hit was the first walk-off infield single in World Series history.

The catcher's heroics spurred Philadelphia on. Howard homered twice in a 10–2 Game 4 rout. Hamels, who

## 10,000 LOSSES

The Phillies are one of the oldest teams in American sports. And given that they have had long periods without success, in 2007 they became the first team in any sport to lose 10,000 games. At the time, they had an all-time record of 8,810–10,000. But after a 15-year period that included lots of wins, the team picked up its 10,000th victory on August 16, 2022. That had been done by only eight teams.

**Closer Brad Lidge, *left,* celebrates the final out of the 2008 World Series with catcher Carlos Ruiz, *right.***

was 4–0 in the postseason, returned for a bizarre Game 5. He allowed two runs in six innings before the game was halted by rain. It took two days for the skies to clear. When play finally resumed, Phillies third baseman Pedro Feliz broke a 3–3 tie on an RBI single in the bottom of the seventh. Closer Brad Lidge came on to close out the game in the ninth. After getting the final out on a strikeout, the righty dropped to his knees and screamed with emotion as players charged out to begin another Philadelphia celebration.

# CHASING ANOTHER TITLE

The next year, the Phillies returned to the World Series but lost in six games to the New York Yankees. Starting in 2009, the Phillies began collecting the league's top pitchers. Superstars like Pedro Martínez, Cliff Lee, Roy Oswalt, and Roy Halladay all joined the team over the next few seasons. Philadelphia reached the NLCS in 2010 and the playoffs again in 2011. But each year, the Phillies came up short.

The 2011 NLDS loss was the unofficial end of the Phillies' golden era. They battled to a .500 record in 2012, but soon they were at the bottom of the NL East. Injuries derailed Howard's promising career, and other members of the World Series core were gone by the mid-2010s. In July 2015, Hamels pitched a no-hitter only to be traded six days later.

The Phillies spent the next several years looking for stars to put them back on top. After the 2018 season, Philadelphia splashed big money to sign former MVP right fielder

## HALLADAY'S HEROICS

The Phillies' 2010 playoff run included an all-time memorable moment. Righty Roy Halladay pitched a no-hitter in a 4–0 victory over the Cincinnati Reds in Game 1 of the NLDS. It was just the second postseason no-hitter in baseball history. The only thing that kept Halladay from a perfect game was a fifth-inning walk. Halladay had previously tossed a perfect game during the 2010 regular season.

Bryce Harper signed a then-record 13-year, $330-million contract with the Phillies on March 2, 2019.

Bryce Harper away from their division rivals, the Washington Nationals. The superstar won MVP again in 2021. A year later he led a powerful lineup on an unlikely run to the World Series. The Phillies jumped out to a 2–1 series lead on the heavily favored Houston Astros.

Houston rallied to take the series. But the Phillies had a young, exciting team and one of the game's biggest stars. Things were looking up in the City of Brotherly Love.

# TIMELINE

**1883**

The Philadelphia Phillies, also known as the Quakers, play their first season as members of the National League.

**1887**

The Phillies move into National League Park, later known as the Baker Bowl, their home for more than 50 years.

**1915**

Behind the pitching of Grover Cleveland Alexander, the Phillies win their first NL title but lose in the World Series.

**1932**

Chuck Klein wins the first MVP in team history and wins the Triple Crown the next season.

**1938**

The team leaves the aging Baker Bowl for the more modern Shibe Park, which they share with the Philadelphia Athletics until that team moves to Kansas City in 1954.

**1950**

The young upstart group of "Whiz Kids" makes a surprising run to the World Series but is swept by the New York Yankees.

**1964**

With a Rookie of the Year campaign from Dick Allen, the Phillies lead the NL for most of the year but collapse in the season's final two weeks.

**1971**

The Phillies play their first season in the multipurpose Veterans Stadium, which they share with the Philadelphia Eagles of pro football.

**1972**

Despite the team's 59–97 record, ace Steve Carlton wins 27 games and earns the first of four Cy Young Awards in a Phillies uniform.

**1980**

Behind an MVP season from third baseman Mike Schmidt, the Phillies break through to the first World Series title in team history.

**1983**

The Phillies reach the World Series again but lose to the Baltimore Orioles in five games.

**1993**

The "Macho Row" Phillies make a worst-to-first run to the World Series but lose in heartbreaking fashion to the Toronto Blue Jays.

**2004**

The Phillies move into Citizens Bank Park, a baseball-only stadium near the site of Veterans Stadium.

**2008**

Led by a dominant playoff performance from pitcher Cole Hamels, the Phillies win a second World Series title. They repeat as NL champs in 2009 but lose the World Series.

**2022**

Behind a powerful lineup led by slugger Bryce Harper, the Phillies reach the World Series before falling 4–2 to the Houston Astros.

# TEAM FACTS

## FRANCHISE HISTORY

Philadelphia Quakers
(1883–89)
Philadelphia Phillies
(1890–1943, 1946– )
Philadelphia Blue Jays
(1944–45)

## WORLD SERIES CHAMPIONSHIPS

1980, 2008

## KEY PLAYERS

Grover Cleveland Alexander
(1911–17, 1930)
Dick Allen (1963–69, 1975–76)
Richie Ashburn (1948–59)
Jim Bunning (1964–67,
1970–71)
Steve Carlton (1972–86)
Darren Daulton (1983,
1985–97)
Roy Halladay (2010–13)
Bryce Harper (2019– )
Ryan Howard (2004–16)

Chuck Klein (1928–33, 1936–39,
1940–44)
John Kruk (1989–94)
Robin Roberts (1948–61)
Jimmy Rollins (2000–14)
Mike Schmidt (1972–89)

## KEY MANAGERS

Dallas Green (1979–81)
Charlie Manuel (2005–13)
Gene Mauch (1960–68)

## HOME STADIUMS

Recreation Park (1883–86)
Baker Bowl (1887–1938)
Also known as: National
League Park (1887–94)
Connie Mack Stadium
(1938–70)
Also known as: Shibe Park
(1938–52)
Veterans Stadium (1971–2003)
Citizens Bank Park (2004– )

## RING IT

For its entire existence, Veterans Stadium had a replica of the Liberty Bell high atop the stands overlooking the field. The 19-foot- (5.8-m) high bell was then relocated to Citizens Bank Park when the team moved in 2004.

## BASEBALL AFTER DARK

Though it took place on the road, the Phillies played in the first night game in MLB history. The Cincinnati Reds hosted the Phillies in a 1935 game at Crosley Field.

## VOICE FROM ABOVE

Starting in 1972, just one voice introduced players at Phillies home games for more than 50 years. Dan Baker began his 51st season as the team's public address announcer at the start of the 2022 season.

## HONORING TUG

Tug McGraw, the Phillies' closer on the 1980 championship team, is the father of country music legend Tim McGraw. The popular pitcher died of cancer in 2004. Tim scattered some of his father's ashes on the pitcher's mound at Citizens Bank Park before Game 3 of the 2008 World Series.

## STEP UP TO THE PLATE

In 2008 Phillies shortstop Jimmy Rollins set an MLB record with 778 plate appearances in a season. The old record had been set by another Phillie, Lenny Dykstra, who batted 773 times in 1993.

# GLOSSARY

**ace**

A team's best starting pitcher.

**batting average**

A player's number of hits divided by the number of at-bats.

**closer**

A pitcher who comes in at the end of a game to secure a win for his team.

**count**

The number of balls and strikes on a batter during an at-bat.

**debut**

First appearance.

**no-hitter**

A complete game in which a team does not allow any hits.

**pennant**

Another name for a league championship; in MLB, it refers to winning either the American or National League championship.

**perfect game**

A complete game in which a team retires every opposing batter and allows no base runners.

**save**

When a relief pitcher comes into a close game and preserves a win.

**walk-off**

Any victory in which the home team scores the winning run in the bottom of the final inning.

# MORE INFORMATION

## BOOKS

Flynn, Brendan. *The MLB Encyclopedia*. Minneapolis, MN: Abdo Publishing, 2022.

Gitlin, Marty. *MLB*. Minneapolis, MN: Abdo Publishing, 2021.

Hewson, Anthony K. *GOATs of Baseball*. Minneapolis, MN: Abdo Publishing, 2022.

## ONLINE RESOURCES

To learn more about the Philadelphia Phillies, please visit **abdobooklinks.com** or scan this QR code. These links are routinely monitored and updated to provide the most current information available.

# ABOUT THE AUTHOR

Anthony K. Hewson is a freelance writer who specializes in writing nonfiction for kids.